A Treadmill Without a Stop Button

A Treadmill Without a Stop Button

by Lauren Pirie

Published by Lauren Pirie in 2023

Publishing services provided by Lumphanan Press

www.lumphananpress.co.uk

ISBN: 978-1-3999-4584-4

Printed & Bound by Imprint Digital, UK

Dedicated to my family and friends

Introduction

Anxiety. We have all experienced it in some form, being anxious for a job interview, meeting new people, a big crowd, the list can go on, but when anxiety completely takes over your life, that is when you are most vulnerable, and it is hard to come out of. Luckily for me, I had the support of my family and friends, because without them I wouldn't be here today to tell you my story and my journey through the deep dark hole that is anxiety.

Growing up I didn't know what anxiety was. I was too young to understand it, but I remember that I was always sick and had a sore tummy. It wasn't until I got into my teens that people started to say you must just be nervous or anxious, it will pass, but it never did. I went to multiple therapists as a young teen in Sweden, where we lived at the time. I was prescribed my first antidepressant at the age of twelve. In my head I was thinking this pill is going to work and take away all my negative thoughts and make me feel happy. I think as a younger person it was easier to just take a pill and not really read too much into it, just that it would help to make me better.

I was put on sertraline 50mg and was on it for ten years, but after time the 50mg wasn't working for me anymore and had worn off. We then upped it to 100mg when I was twenty and then we upped it again to 150mg and it worked so much better. I was, during these years, often non-compliant with taking my medication and would stop and start. Starting it again would then bring back the constant headaches, insomnia, feeling sick, so please take your medications, regularly. They are helping you.

Please believe me when I say that when you start on antidepressants, it takes time for them to kick into your system. The first two weeks you will feel that your anxiety is really high. You might feel irritated and that you can't sleep, but stick with it because after you have hit the two-week mark, you will start to feel okay again. I think we panic and say this is getting worse, it's not working and then stop taking the medication. It is working. It just takes time for your body to adjust. It may be that medication isn't right for you and that's okay. There are plenty of other things that you could try. I know I have.

Chapter 1

Accident Forms

Even though I didn't know what anxiety was at a young age and I most certainly didn't know I suffered from it, just that everyone else did, I often woke up with a sore tummy in the mornings, thinking I was really ill. I would be sick most mornings, but in actual fact I was just super duper anxious. I'd cry every morning begging my mum not to take me to school. I hated school, the teachers, the work, but I had a good group of friends at the time, which made it easier to go every day. The only thing with school friends is that you do drift apart. Friends move to different countries or change schools and the school switches up the classes when it's a start of a new term. I did find that hard because when you are so young, you feel like your friends back then are going to be your friends for the rest of your life, but that might not be the case. I have had a lot of different friend groups in my lifetime. Only a few people I could truly call my best friends are still in my life. I also found being a girl and having my friend group being mainly females, there would always be fights or dramas. Someone would fall out with someone. That meant we couldn't talk to them. Now I think of it as very childish, but like I said, we were only children and teens. I don't really think much of it now.

If someone wants to be in my life, I would be able to see that. I try for so long and then if it's not working, there isn't much point in trying. Sometimes friendships can be one way and that isn't fair. You put so much time and effort into trying. You start to overthink things.

Do they still want to be friends?

Is it me?

Did I say something wrong?

How am I going to fix this?

That's the thing, maybe some friendships aren't meant to be fixed and that is okay. There are a lot of people we will meet in this world that will come and go, but the ones who stay are the ones to keep close.

I struggled in school with most subjects but also found it hard to ask for help because I didn't want to be singled out, which was silly because I needed the help so bad and struggled every day. I wouldn't understand what the lesson was about, or I had forgotten what the teacher had said. I would come to my mam, and she would ask what I had for homework, and I wouldn't have a clue. I used to go to the bathroom a lot, not to use it but to just waste some time. My friends must have thought I had toilet issues.

I think for me what makes my anxiety high is anticipation of what the day has in store, not knowing what will happen. For instance, like going to a birthday party or waiting in the doctors' waiting room. You don't know what will happen until you get there and once there realise that actually it isn't that scary. I tell myself that before going, but my head always conjures up the worst-case scenarios. Like the doctor is going to tell me I'm going to die, or no one will play with me at the party. Our minds have funny ways of making us feel scared and anxious about things. If we try and change the way we think, we might have better outcomes. I know that's easier said than done.

For me in school I often used to get the attention of the teachers or the pupil support assistants by telling them I was not feeling well or had a sore leg/head or any part of my body if I'm honest, just to try to get sent home. Most times it would work, but sometimes it wouldn't, and I would get sent home at the end of the day with accident forms. My poor mum would probably get five a week. I had a fair collection going on. I think that should have signalled some warning signs from the school, but no one really picked up on it. In school, there were many pupil support assistants, so I would go to a different one each time. I feel that I was trying to reach out in some way to show that I wasn't coping, even though I didn't know it at the time.

I did find ways to distract myself from my sore tummy. I would write down stories about all different things, fairies, crimes, life. It was my way of keeping a diary. I had a great imagination, and still do.

We also experience anxiety from our loved ones. We pick up on their emotions and it rubs off on us. We do learn traits from our loved ones. It's a good thing and a bad thing.

I never went to the doctors about my anxiety when I was little because back then I don't think it was a big thing. I think everyone around me just thought I was a nervous child. If I had maybe had early intervention, things might have been different, but we can't dwell in the past. There isn't any point. The more we dig deeper into our past, the further away we are from moving forward into the future.

I remember in school there was one teacher that I liked because she took notice and praised me when I did something good rather than get angry if I didn't understand or was too slow to answer the question. I work in a school now and really make an effort to praise the children when they have done good. I feel that it really motivates them and keeps them focused and also just makes them feel confident. There isn't any point getting angry at a child just because they don't understand and are finding it hard. I'm lucky enough to work in a school with such great staff that look after all their kids so well.

When I do accident forms at work, it brings back memories of when I was in school and I really take notice of how the child is, if it's serious or if the child might just want a little attention. It also gives you that chance to talk to the child and actively listen.

Never did I think I would be working in a school considering how I really didn't like it, but it's different when you are older.

If I could go back to my younger self, I would tell her that it will be a crazy ride, but we make it through every time because we are strong and are able to handle everything thrown at us. My Swedish auntie Eva told me when I have a really big panic attack that I go back to being a scared little girl and she wasn't worried about the strong, capable twenty-seven-year-old adult sitting in front of her but the little girl I had reverted to. When I go into a big panic, I turn into a terrified little girl, who feels so trapped. Recently when I have had a panic attack, I speak to my inner self and try to calm myself down by speaking kindly to that little girl and block out all the negative thoughts that are running around in my head. Your inner child is the one who is hurting when we speak negatively about ourselves. Think about what you are saying. Would you say that to a small child?

Sometimes challenging your thoughts and realising that they aren't true and aren't going to happen will also help. I get so consumed with all the thoughts that go through my brain. An average person thinks between 60,000–80,000 thoughts per day. Can you imagine someone who is an overthinker and has anxiety? It honestly feels like your brain will explode.

I managed to get through school with some good and bad experiences. I left school at fifteen and I do regret it a little bit, but if I hadn't left school, then I wouldn't have done all the other things I have managed to do already in my life. I went on to study floristry and have been a qualified florist for ten years this year.

When I was younger, I think it was so much easier. I didn't have a phone to google all my symptoms or social media to compare my life with other people's. Limiting my time on my phone has helped me, even sometimes deleting some of the apps off my phone so I don't have the choice to open them. I even deleted Safari because it was getting to the point that every time I'd get a new medication, I would google all the symptoms that come along with it and would convince myself I had them all.

I would then phone my GP in tears and tell them I need to change medication. All medications come with side effects, but you rarely experience even a quarter of them and if you do experience some, they only last a short period of time. As someone with anxiety I found it hard because I didn't want anything to make me feel worse, but they are there to help. It just takes time. I will be talking more about social media in Chapter 2.

I had so many strong women in my life growing up and always looked up to them. Having a strong support system is key. Us women need to look out for one another.

When you experience anxiety, your body is going into fight or flight mode and all the adrenaline is going at once. We are supposed to have it because if we didn't, we would be in danger and not know what is safe or not. It can also go the other way and get really overwhelming and can lead us into a state of panic. It's our body's way of coping with the challenging battles in life.

For me anxiety is a silent, scary, horrible thing to go through and many people can hide their feelings really well. It's awful to think that they could be going through the hardest time in their lives and we don't even know it. Check up on your loved ones. You could be the only person in their life and they probably need you the most right now. Be kind and gentle. You might not know what to say and that's okay, just let the person know that you are here for them. It's all they need. I know from experience. Even having someone in the room with you makes you feel safe and loved.

You will get blips along the road. Every day won't be a good day, but you need to try and turn your not-so-good day into a better one. Whether it be taking a shower, taking your dog for a walk, doing some colouring or writing in a diary. Putting your thoughts onto paper is a really good way to relieve your stress and worries. Try doing at least one thing for you. Rome wasn't built in a day; it will take time and that's fine. You can't cure your mental health, but you can work on it and not let it take over. Get the right help and don't stop until you feel that you have been seen by the right people.

It will get easier and there is a light at the end of the tunnel and however deep your dark hole is, you will get back up again and get stronger every time.

Chapter 2

Social media

Social media wasn't a part of my life when I was growing up. I didn't enter it until my late teens. Sometimes I wish some of the apps weren't created. I love them for staying in touch with family and friends but dislike them because non-stop comparing yourself to everyone else is physically and mentally draining. I was addicted to this when I was younger and have to stop myself even now. Deleting some social media sites can help in so many ways: better sleep, no non-stop scrolling, no constant checking. It becomes an addiction and it's hard not to just pick up your phone and open all the apps.

I didn't realise for a long time that social media was causing me anxiety. If I had posted something, I would keep checking how many people had liked the picture or post. I would even delete the post if I didn't think it did well, which is really sad because I should have allowed myself to post whatever I wanted and not cared if it got likes or not. It took me such a long time to figure that out and is still something I sometimes struggle with today. I found it hard not to compare other people's lives with my own seemingly very boring life, but I did learn that the things we share are only a small fraction of our lives and definitely not the full picture. I imagine that their lives are nowhere near as perfect as they make them out to be online.

Having the internet at your fingertips can be a bad thing. As I mentioned before, regarding my anxiety, I would google all of my symptoms and my brain would convince myself that I had every single one. The symptoms would then just escalate, which would lead me into a state of panic that was very hard to get out of.

A positive thing about the internet is that there are lots of resources and groups that you can join. Sometimes it can feel a bit of an overload, but for me listening to podcasts helps or looking up positive quotes.

When I get into a dark place, I find it hard to connect with people. If someone has texted or phoned me, it can take me a while to message back. When I'm in a rut, even if I have people around me reaching out, I can still feel lonely.

I love taking photos and having them on my phone and going back and scrolling through them. It makes me feel happy. A picture lasts a lifetime and has so many memories.

I do follow a lot of people on Instagram who inspire me and sometimes looking through their pages helps.

One person who inspires me is my auntie Eva and she has a great social media following and has helped so many couples. Eva is an Imago therapist. She has written books and does her own podcasts. Eva is the one who inspired me to write this book. When I was going through a very tough time, with daily panic attacks, Eva was over from Sweden for a visit, and she knew exactly how to calm me down. Sometimes when I have a panic attack, I can hear her voice saying open your eyes, look around; if you don't, you will go back into that deep dark hole. A panic attack isn't dangerous, but it definitely feels like you are dying. The worst thing that could happen is that you faint and then you will start breathing properly again.

Try and ground yourself. Try doing the 5-4-3-2-1 coping technique.

5. Find 5 things you can see in the room, that can be the tv, the dog, a family member.

4. Find 4 things you can touch. It could be your bed cover, the sofa underneath you, your hair.

3. Listen for 3 things you can hear, could be the cars passing by, your belly rumbling.

2. Find 2 things that you can smell, maybe your perfume, fresh cut grass, fresh brewed coffee.

1. Find 1 thing you can taste. What does it taste like in your mouth? Could be toothpaste, your lunch, coffee.

There is no right or wrong way of doing this, just make sure you start from 5 and work down to 1. Try it a few times. It might take a few goes before you feel more grounded. Go out for a walk and try it – there are so many more things to see and smell and hear.

Times have changed since I was little. I didn't use the internet as much as I do now. I use my phone for everything, checking restaurant menus, directions, time, calculator, the list is endless. It was much easier back then because I didn't have a phone and played outside and was more adventurous. I didn't need the time because I just waited until the street lights came on and that would be my time to go in. We rely so much on our phones that, God forbid, when we lose them or break them, it's the end of the world.

The internet is different now with new apps coming into play, for instance TikTok; you can watch absolutely anything on there. Children can make accounts and watch some crazy things because TikTok decides what comes up on your feed and that could be anything. It can be very unsafe. It then becomes very addictive. What would have been ten minutes of scrolling could end up being two hours because you get so consumed. I deleted the app because I saw a lot of negative stuff and I didn't like the way it made me feel. Don't get me wrong; I do love when someone sends me a funny video, but I think for me it's better not to use it.

I do love using YouTube to listen to calming music before bed or when I feel a little anxious. I find that this calms me down and slows my heartrate a bit. It allows me to focus on the music and not my negative thoughts racing round my head at the time. There are so many videos to choose from. I just search for sleep music or calming mediation.

There are also really good influencers on YouTube that discuss anxiety and other mental health issues. The most recent person that I have been following is Dr Alex. I find him easy to watch as he has a calming voice. He is a mental health ambassador, doctor and has also suffered from anxiety. He isn't afraid to show it. I love his work. He has recently started up a stomp cast, which is when he brings in a different person every Monday and goes for a stomp (walk). You can listen on Spotify. I really enjoy listening while walking up to work in the morning. He is raising awareness and helping us with helpful tips and advice. Alex is trying to stop the stigma of taking antidepressants. You shouldn't have to be afraid or feel criticised for taking medications if it's going to benefit your mental health. I'm standing with him. #postyourpill

You get a sense of belonging on social media. You post a picture; you get the likes. It makes you feel happy for a little while, but the vicious circle continues. You start to question yourself. Should I post it? Why did they get more likes? I don't look good in this picture.

When taking time off social media, it feels good for a bit, but then you get the fear of missing out. Wondering what everyone else is up to. Then that resorts to you going back on your phone and checking all your apps. I can see why I sometimes think that social media does cause some mental health issues, especially for our younger generation. When there is a filter applied to the online world, our younger generation finds it hard to know what is real and what isn't, which comes at a difficult time for them physically and emotionally. Back in the day, teens would read pop magazines and compare themselves to models and take quizzes. Now we have full access to everything that is on the web. I do compare myself to a lot of people. I think especially us women are sometimes our own biggest enemies.

There is also a huge sense of empowerment from women online. I sometimes have a look at people's comments on their posts. Most of them are positive, but you get the odd few that are just ridiculous. Online trolls shouldn't have the power to do that. I give props to Instagram because you can limit comments on your post or completely turn them off. People don't think before they comment. That comment could ruin that person's day. If you have thick skin, you can brush it off, but for someone who is having a hard time mentally, that is adding extra crap that they don't need.

Chapter 3

Life stories

I remember the first day of my new school in Sweden like it was yesterday. I had set out my outfit on my bed the night before. In Sweden they don't have uniforms, which is good and bad because it's great having the choice of what to wear but also worrying in case you get judged on what you are wearing.

I woke up super early and I couldn't have breakfast I was so nervous.

What are they going to think of me?

Are they going to think I sound weird?

Do they speak English?

Will I make new friends?

All these thoughts were spiralling around in my head. A lot of what-ifs.

Before heading out the door, I ran to the toilet and was sick. My tummy was hurting so much, and I was really tired since I didn't sleep very well the night before.

Mum was driving us to school that morning in our big black car. Our house was in the middle of the woods. Trees for days. Sweden is such a beautiful country.

Mum drove us for the first couples of weeks and then we started to take the bus to school on our own, which I will come back to.

During the journey there I didn't say much. We drove up the hill to the school and walked down to the entrance. My hands were sweating, my heart was beating fast, my cheeks had gone rosy, I felt so sick.

We got to my classroom door and we were late. All I could think was that I'm going to walk in there, and they will all be staring at me. I said goodbye to my mum and said hello to my new teacher. The classroom door opened and, as I had expected, the whole class turned around and looked at me. The teacher took me to my seat, which was the furthest seat from the classroom door. The walk to my seat felt like it was taking forever. I got to sit beside a lovely girl called Hannah who I'd met before on my visits before starting. She was so welcoming and tried to speak English. Across from me was Emma. I didn't know it then, but she would become my best friend. We were and still are inseparable. She means the world to me.

As the day went on, my nerves had settled down a bit. I didn't eat much at lunchtime because I wasn't hungry and also initially, I thought the food didn't taste nice. I got used to the new foods that I tried and slowly began to like them.

The bell went for home time, and I went to get my bag and walked up the hill to meet Mum, who was waiting in the car. Mum asked how I got on; I said it was okay and I have to do it all over again tomorrow. Although I had done a day, having to do another one was scary.

Each day did get easier and easier, and I started to make friends.

It took me over a year to learn Swedish, but I think it definitely helped that I went to a Swedish school. It's nice when I visit back home in Sweden that I can speak the language. You feel a sense of belonging. I feel like Sweden has a different way of living compared to us. How they live, their fashion sense. The forests, the rivers. Everywhere you look it is breath-taking.

The thing I did struggle with was seasonal depression. When it gets to wintertime and the mornings are dark and the nights are dark, you do tend to feel more down. The temperature starts to drop. Where we lived was in the middle of nowhere. It was just pitch black most of the time. Having my brothers Kieran, Kyle, Jake and Noah there helped because we kept each other entertained.

The experience of moving to Sweden was a good one. It has helped me through life and If I didn't go to that school, I wouldn't have met my best friend Emma. We wouldn't have made such great memories together and many more memories to come.

Emma doesn't know it, but she has helped me through a lot of things in my life. Even now since we live in different countries, when we do get to see each other, it's like we have never been apart. I could tell her anything and she wouldn't judge. She may not be going through anything that I've experienced, but she is always there to try and understand and sends lot of love.

Back to taking the bus to school. It was a scary experience going on the bus without an adult, but I did have my four brothers with me. My brother Jake went to the same school as me and my brothers Kieran and Kyle went to another school in town. Noah went to nursery.

I remember when Mum told us that we would be taking the bus to school, and I thought to myself, that can't be right, I'm only ten years old. The thoughts that I had were racing through my mind.

What happens if I get kidnapped?

What happens if I miss my bus and never get home?

What happens if I get lost on the journey home?

I had so many thoughts at that time, especially when I was nervous for something.

I think it didn't help having to walk to the bus in the middle of nowhere and in the dark. This made it ten times scarier.

The only thing I was excited for was getting my own bus pass. I thought it was cool because you went on the bus, and you would put your bus pass through the machine and it would pop back up and give you your card back. It also told you how much you had left.

It was also nice when my brother Kyle would share his iPod with me, and I would get to listen to his music.

I would get worried in case I'd miss the bus stop on the way home from school or be late for my bus or even miss it in the morning, which actually happened so many times and I had to walk back to the house and ask Mum to take me. At the end of the day, missing the bus isn't a worst-case scenario. Maybe for a little girl it is, but it can always be fixed.

I get where my mam was coming from. It did give me independence and I'm really good with directions and not scared to go on any transport by myself.

Once I'd got the hang of going on the bus and getting into a routine of getting to the bus stop in time with my brothers and waiting for the bus to arrive, it got easier for me. I wasn't scared of going on the bus anymore. You've got to do things that scare you a little. You feel so much happier and confident afterwards. If you don't manage the first, second or even third attempt, it's important to keep trying and you will succeed.

I know maybe going on a bus isn't a big deal for some

people, but for a ten-year-old who had just moved to a different country and didn't know the language, it was pretty darn scary.

When I was younger, I loved going to my friend's house to play. We would always phone and ask if we could come over and we would play for hours and hours, but when it got to the end of our play time, my friends would always ask for a sleepover. I kept thinking please don't ask your mum. Most of the time it would be a no because it would be a school night and I would sigh with relief but then pretend to look sad for my friends. I was so scared of staying over at their house. I would miss my mum and my bed, and I didn't feel safe if I wasn't at home.

I eventually had a sleepover at my friend's house, and I was crying to my mum beforehand and begging her to let me stay at home with my brothers. My two older brothers were being allowed to stay at home alone as Mum had to stay over somewhere that night.

I had my bag packed with my favourite teddy bear and my pjs and toothbrush. I walked round to my friend's house and she opened the door with a big smile and my nerves settled a bit. I was calmed by the fact that we had a long time until we had to go to bed. We went to her room and played with some of her Barbies. We had supper and watched some tv. The time went by so quick, and suddenly her mum shouted that it was time for bed and immediately my heart sank. I could feel my eyes filling up. I kept saying to myself over and over in my head that I could do this, that I was brave.

We went upstairs and brushed our teeth and put on our pjs and got into bed. We chatted for a bit and she then turned off the light. It was time to sleep. My tummy was doing jumping jacks. All I could think of was wanting to go home to my own bed. I tried closing my eyes and counting sheep or counting to one hundred. I just lay there waiting for the night to be over.

I slowly opened my eyes, and the room was bright. I must have been able to fall asleep. I think all the stress and worry had tired me out. I was so proud of myself. I did it. I had many sleepovers after that and became the one who kept asking if I could sleep over.

I put myself out of my comfort zone and I felt scared and anxious, but at the end of the day, what was the worst that could happen? I'd get upset and have to go home. I'm glad I managed, because I had faced one of my fears and gained more confidence.

I had lots of life-changing moments in my life, as I'm sure many people have. It is a part of life. We have a lot of change. Everything is not perfect all the time and that's okay. We make mistakes – we are only human at the end of the day. Tomorrow is never guaranteed, so live for today.

The thing that would help make me feel safe and comfortable when I was in a new place was taking my favourite teddy and my own pillows. I'd make sure I had my phone at the side of my bed and sleep with the door slightly open. I still do all those things.

We've only got one life and we need to live it to the fullest. Enjoy the happy moments, go through the hard and sad times but come out of it stronger than ever.

Life is a scary rollercoaster at times but also one hell of a beautiful journey.

Chapter 4

In the now

This chapter will be the hardest to write, but I want to share it to show people who are going through similar things as me that there are good times as well as bad. I know because I got out of the worst time. Over six months ago my life turned upside down. In all, 2021 was an okay year. There were some stresses and some nervous times but nothing too extreme. At the end of the year, I became very sick. I tested for Covid, but it came back negative. This all happened during Christmas time. My PCR test took six days to come back. I spent Christmas and New Year on my own with my dog Freya. My family were in Sweden at the time.

That two weeks gave me plenty of time to think and be in my head. I was overthinking everything. I started being sick in the morning because of my anxiety. I was phoning my mum every day. My mental health was just getting worse. I was alone in the house and wasn't allowed out in case I had Covid. I felt stuck.

A couple of weeks later and 2022 arrived. My family came back from Sweden, and they had to quarantine and wait for their tests to come back. Before work started, I had one day to chat to Mum, but I don't think it was enough. Mum drove me back to my flat so I could get organised for my work the next day. I woke up in the morning with such a strange feeling. I got ready for work and went out the door. When I got to work, I felt so emotional and as if I was out of my body. People were speaking to me, but I was unable to take in anything they were saying. I managed to get through the day and went home to my flat. Then the panic just got worse and worse. I phoned my mum and broke down and said I'm scared, and I don't know what's happening. Mum had phoned Robin (my stepdad) because she couldn't pick me up as she was still at work. Robin picked me up and I was in tears. Mum came home from work and we cuddled, and I cried, and we had a chat. I stayed over and from then on it just went downhill. I gave up my flat and moved in with my family. Now I look back, it was the best decision. I was being sick every morning. I had lost a lot of weight. I wasn't sleeping and we know how we get when we haven't slept. It isn't good at all for our mental health. My panic attacks became more physical. I was feeling so out of control. I didn't know what to do, and my family didn't know what to do either.

I was phoning helplines and 111 on a daily basis, just trying to find the right help.

If you phone 111, you can speak to a trained mental health professional, who will speak to you and make sure you are safe. They will try and find the right help for you.

At the time my GP practice closed down and we had to be moved to a new one. This was really nerve-racking for me because the new GPs knew nothing about me and when I'd phone up I would get a different GP each time.

My many phone calls to the GP resulted in me being put on ten different antidepressants in the space of six months. The side effects were many and horrible as I didn't really give any of the medications a chance to start working. I did finally manage to stick to one tablet that I have been on for three months now. It takes time. It won't get better overnight. Just stick with it.

I had the worst thoughts during the bad times. I had written goodbye letters to my family because I thought I couldn't see a way out. I stopped myself from going through with it and phoned 111. I got an emergency appointment with a mental health hospital and got to chat with them there. When I spoke to the mental health team on 111, they referred me to a community mental health nurse, and I think that it has been such a positive experience. She has helped me in so many ways. I am lucky to have her support. We have weekly or fortnightly chats. We are also working on cognitive behaviour therapy. I think I will really benefit in the long run.

When I think back on it now, I definitely regret it and am grateful that I didn't go through with it because I am at a more positive part

of my life, and I feel a lot happier. Even though I still have sad days where I don't want to go out or take a shower, they aren't as bad as they were. I think when we get into that state of feeling like there isn't much more I can do or anyone else can do, you do start to think, what's the point? Luckily for me when I do get into that head space, I think of my family and how they would feel, what they would have to go through, and then my mind switches and I try and distract myself.

During those six months I was off work. I was devastated because I love my job and I am good at it. I work so hard with the children I work with and help them through their school experiences. I love my work colleagues; they make the job more fun.

I am so grateful for the staff at the school. The management especially. Their support has helped me in a lot of ways. Their kindness to me has been lovely. I can't wait to get back to work after the summer holidays.

Each day I see a little bit of myself coming back and I know that I might not be one hundred percent myself again and that is okay because I think I am gaining a better version instead.

For me what really helped was keeping a diary and writing down everything that I felt in the moment. It does really help. Then when I look back on it, I feel happier because of how far I have come. A lot like writing this book. It has been very therapeutic.

During those awful times, I gave up on everything I loved doing, like baking and flower arranging. Even now I still haven't had the urge to pick up my apron or arrange some flowers, but I know that day will come and when it does, it will be amazing. I didn't see any of my friends and found it hard to reply to messages. I deleted Facebook and Instagram for a while because I would get sad seeing everyone else happy whilst I was in the biggest black hole ever. That's now changed. I now get so much joy seeing everyone happy. Seeing their children grow or seeing photos of weddings and birthdays. There is so much to celebrate in this life.

About a month ago I started to have seizures. I was aware of what was happening; my eyes would go black at times and my whole body would seize up. It was such a scary time. My little brother Noah was there during the first one because my mum and stepdad Robin had gone away for the night. I had collapsed to the floor and the seizure started. I lost control of my bladder and bowels.

I felt so embarrassed. Noah phoned Mum to come home and they did. I had another four seizures. We didn't phone an ambulance, because at the time Robin didn't think it was epilepsy and had been timing them. They had only lasted for about two to five minutes but felt like a lifetime.

I got referred to a neurology clinic. I got an appointment to see a neurologist and met a great consultant who asked a lot of questions. Mum had recorded my seizures, which was helpful for the consultant. He was eighty percent sure that it wasn't epilepsy, but to be sure I was referred for an EEG scan and an MRI to rule out anything else.

I was diagnosed with FND, functional neurology disorder. FND is a medical condition where there is a problem with the nervous system and how the brain sends and receives signals. I lose control of my bowel movements and bladder. I find it hard to walk and talk afterwards. It feels like my legs aren't mine, my brain feels worse for wear. Extreme tiredness. Pins and needles in my hands and feet. Pain all over my body. FND seizures are non-epileptic and don't need medication. The main beneficial help for FND is cognitive behaviour therapy, which I will be starting soon. I'm glad I have a diagnosis; I can now work on keeping my anxiety low and stress levels even lower to help myself from having any more seizures. Since getting my diagnosis I have joined different groups on Facebook, trying to get some answers and different insights into other people's stories on how they deal with FND.

I am grateful for my family and friends and especially my Mam. She has gone through everything with me and she didn't give up on me. She was there every step of the way. She answered the phone every time I was upset and panicking. She always said she felt so frustrated because she knew she couldn't help, but she was helping just by being there for me and often that was what helped me through. She slept in my bed with me because I had panic attacks during the night. She rubbed my back and held my hair when I was being sick. Held me every time I fainted. She made sure I was eating and drinking enough. I can't thank her enough and no number of cuddles will do, but Mam, if you are reading this, I love you so much and I'm lucky to have you in my life. You are my rock, my best friend.

And for my Dad, I love you to the moon and back! I will always be your little girl. Thank you for always being there for me, you mean the world to me.

I am proud of how far I have come when often I felt as if I was making no progress at all. I'm also grateful that I can share my story and hopefully help at least one person. Dark days will sometimes come around, but it is how we deal with them and, more importantly, how we put effort into changing the day around by trying to do at least one thing that will make us happy. Changing the narrative one day at a time. You won't wake up and find everything is back to normal, but you can make small changes and slowly work on yourself.

Never be afraid to ask for help and don't stop until you get the right help. Never feel embarrassed either. A lot of people are going through similar things as you. The person across from or beside you could be going through a really hard time. When I was looking for help, I did hit a lot of dead ends and didn't think anyone wanted to help me, but I realised that I didn't need anyone to save me. I could save myself. I think I was waiting for a knight in shining armour to come and protect me from all evil, but that wasn't going to happen. I needed to do this for myself. I picked myself up from rock bottom multiple times and kept going.

Chapter 5

Moving forward

So, what's next for me? The world is my oyster. I'm looking forward to seeing friends and being more social. I have given up alcohol, which I think is a good thing. I don't need to drink alcohol to have a good time. I get a sugar high from the mocktails. I'm hoping to be back to work by the end of the summer holidays and looking forward to hearing the children call my name, Miss Pirie.

I'm taking each day as it comes. I know it's not going to be easy, but I won't give up on happiness. Life is too short to be worrying unnecessarily.

I will continue with my psychiatrist and work on myself and my techniques to help with my anxiety and FND. If you are seeing someone for your mental health, please stick with them or if they aren't a right fit for you, keep trying to find the perfect one. At the end of the day, it's your mental health on the line.

I'm going to start up my hobbies again, start doing the

things I love to do.

It may seem when you have hit rock bottom that your life is over, but it's not. You've hit rock bottom and the only way is back up. If you fall again, you pick yourself right back up and keep going. Lean on the support offered from your family and friends or even your health care professional. Take time for you. Have a rest day, have a mental health day. Treat yourself to a coffee, meet up with a friend in the park. Your life isn't over; it's just starting.

I'm focusing on me and not thinking about what other people think. For a long time, I would worry about what people thought of me or if they didn't like me. I would stress out so much about it. I worried if I would be judged. I never really stood up for myself when I was younger, but now I think I am more confident in voicing my opinion and I don't care what others think.

As we all know, most of the stresses and worries we had as a child are replaced by a whole new set as we head into adult life. But I feel we are more capable as adults to face these and conquer them. We tend to work too hard until we burn out and then find it almost physically and mentally impossible to get out of that situation. We humans work until our glass is empty and we then keep on working, never filling up our glass until something (usually our mental health) has to give. You need to refill that glass, so rest, recharge those batteries, look after yourself so you are able to deal with what life throws at you.

I have made a lot of mistakes in my life and wrong choices and that is okay, we are only human, and we aren't going to be perfect all the time. We learn from our mistakes and grow from them.

Keep your days busy. I find it harder during the summer holidays because my work allows me the whole time off. Six to seven weeks. This is amazing I hear you say, but it's a lot of time to fill. It doesn't mean you have to be with friends every day. I'm happy in my own company when I'm in a good mindset, but I always make sure I get out of the house for an hour or two. I like to window shop and walk round town and just people watch. Distracting the mind and getting good sensory input will really help in the long run. If we stay at home in our pyjamas with the curtains closed sitting in a dark room and hiding from the world, our fears and anxieties will start to manifest, and this will definitely not have a positive outcome. We are then letting our mental health win. By all means accept the fact that there are days when your mental health might be taking a wee dip, but try not to stay in that place long term or it will be so much harder to come out of.

Moving forward is scary, but don't listen to those

voiding thoughts. Try and push yourself and make that day count. Each day gets better, and you will have setbacks. Believe me, I have had a few and I'm still having them. Each time you fall you get back up even stronger.

Having gone through a lot of things in my life and a lot of change, it has moulded the person I am today. Even though the last six months have been the hardest, I am still here writing this book and telling my story. I hope I might be able to help at least one person and make them feel that they aren't alone. Mental health can feel like the loneliest place in the world. It can be hard for some people to understand what you are going through because they haven't experienced severe mental health issues, but you can educate them, tell them how you feel and if they show no interest, then, well, perhaps they shouldn't be part of your journey. Some people find it hard to deal with other people's emotions. I totally understand this. I think they might find it hard to see their friend in pain and don't know what to do to help. My advice is just be there for them. You don't have to speak, just listen or do something to take their mind off their thoughts. Do the things that you guys liked to do.

Distraction is key and keeping yourself busy. Having a plan for the day or a routine to get you started and on the right track again. Everything starts with baby steps. You're not going to climb a mountain. Start small and everything will start to ease again.

My favourite thing to do when feeling low is, if it is raining outside, to open my window wide and sit on my chair with a cup of tea and my dog Freya on my lap and my phone set on do not disturb. Just listening to the rain. Best feeling ever.

Take care of your gut. A lot of what we eat contributes to our anxiety. Having IBS and figuring out what triggers I have when it comes to food has really helped. The morning is when I'm most anxious, so I tend to eat something that isn't high in sugar but is also going to keep me going for the rest of the day. I might have some Special K or bran flakes, or just some toast with butter. Always keep your body hydrated. Start your day with a glass of water.

Little bits of happiness make me feel so much better. It doesn't have to be a big thing; it can just be a bar of chocolate or a hug from a loved one or seeing your dog in the morning. Little joys.

Living with anxiety &
what we can do to help ourselves

Go for a walk and listen to a podcast.

Meet up with a friend or family member for some lunch. Speak to your guidance counsellor in school. They can help with a lot of things that you are struggling with, like your mental health, bullying or even family problems.

Speak to your GP and if you don't feel that you are connecting well with them, you can ask to change GP. Keep trying until it feels right.

If you need someone to talk to but don't want to speak face to face, there a lot of helpline where you can talk to a trained volunteer.

If it is an emergency, please phone 999.

Open up to someone you trust. You might have to open up to a few people before the right one comes along and you just connect. I can think of a few friends that I can just chat and chat to and they understand and get me.

Speak with your manager at work if it's to do with work and you feel you need some help. Don't hesitate to have a chat with them. I'm glad I did.

Have a TLC day, buy some facemasks, run yourself a bath. Paint your nails. Buys lots of snacks or for me I love buying a melon pot and melting chocolate to dip. Find a good Netflix film or series and binge watch it. Do something for you for once.

Look into starting a new hobby, whether it be an exercise class or sewing class. There are so many classes and activities to join. You just need to pick one and be brave enough to go. If it's too overwhelming to go to a class and meet people, there are a lot of online courses you can start off with and then gradually build up to in-person one instead.

If you have a pet, cuddle them. They can sense your emotions. My dog Freya is amazing with me. She doesn't know how much she has helped. Take care of your pets. Give them the same love that they give you.

Yoga and meditation can help for some. I did find it hard to start with. Trying to focus on my breathing and do the moves correctly is challenging but stick with it and it is such a rewarding form of exercise.

Listen to relaxing music or your favourite podcasts.

Switch off from the world that is the internet. Take a few hours without your phone, laptop. The world isn't going anywhere. You won't miss anything.

Try journaling or simply writing down your thoughts as the pop up. Get it on paper so it is out of your mind.

Cold water swimming is a really beneficial activity. It resets the mind, making you feel refreshed and amazing. My mam is a pro at it. We all wear wetsuits, but no, not my mam; she wears just a swimming costume in the cold North Sea. If you don't want to be bashed around by the waves, maybe try a cold shower for thirty seconds and then build it up. Do it in the morning to start your day right.

One thing that does really help for me is baking. I did lose the joy for it but have started to get it back. It has helped with my mental health. Buying the ingredients and having a recipe to follow and then making the finished product that you can share is very therapeutic for me.

Take medication, if that is right for you. Please follow your instincts. It may work for you; it may not. Speak with your GP. They are there to help and advise you to make the right choice.

Last thing, enjoy the small wins and keep those close to you because previously they could have been the hardest things to face. Be proud of how far you have come, how far you have grown. You have come through so many challenges in life so far and I'm sure there will be more, but you are strong, and you can face them.

* * *

So that's my story and some advice for navigating the dark and scary rollercoaster that is anxiety, but after the storm the sun comes out and then a rainbow.

I wanted to write a book for me and for anyone who is going through a tough time.

I am hoping this book might support or provide advice

for someone who needs to help one of their friends or family members. You have got this and anything else that comes your way.

Be strong! Be brave! Be you!

Thank you for reading my stories. I hope this book gives you a little hope for the future. Tough times never last. You will get through this. I believe in you!

Thanks

For my family, without you lot I would not have got through this. I love you all so much.

Mam, Robin.

Dad, Tracey.

Gran, Granda.

Kieran, Kyle, Jake, Noah, Freya.

Auntie Nicola, Uncle Ross, cousins Chloe, Caitlin.

Megan, Shannen and Jude Geddes.

Billy, Stuart and Rhian.

Faster (Auntie) Eva, Sven, Anders, Nicholas, Zoe (AKA the Berlander family).

Emma (best friend), I love you so much. You mean the world to me.

To my work friends, you guys know who you are, you make my day brighter. We are a team.

Gemma and Rachel (my best friends), I love you both. I'm grateful to have you two in my life.

Simona (a very special friend, who I love dearly).

Nicola Milne (lovely friend who just gets it and understands).

Emily Hughes (dear friend, who has been there for me when times are hard and have amazing memories with.

Sorry I if I missed anyone out, would write all your names if I could but that would be a book in itself.

Together we will fight mental health. Thank you for reading.

Love Lauren x